TABLE OF CONTENTS

I. Laying the Foundations of Financial Independence

II. The Power of Setting Goals – A Woman's Vision for Prosperity

III. The Wise Way to Budget – A Guided Approach for Women

IV. Strategic Saving – A Woman's Guide to Building Wealth

V. Investing for The Future – A Woman's Financial Empowerment

VI. Making Your Money Work for You – A Woman's Guide to Financial Independence

VII. Mindful Spending – Nurturing Financial Awareness for Women

VIII Building Multiple Income Streams – A Woman's Path to Financial Resilience

CHAPTER I

Laying the Foundations of Financial Independence

"*Investing should be like watching paint dry or grass grow. If you want excitement, take $800 and go to Las Vegas.*" —Paul Samuelson, economist, reimagined for our narrative.

Smart Money Habits: A Woman's Toolkit for Financial Freedom

Financial habits are the bedrock of a secure future, the silent guardians of prosperity. They are the practices, standards, and values that guide our daily financial decisions. For women, especially, these habits are not just routines but lifelines to independence and empowerment.

Consider Lisa, who after years of living paycheck to paycheck, decided to embark on a journey of financial education. By embracing the principles of smart money management, she transformed her relationship with money, paving her way toward a future where she no longer fears unexpected expenses.

The Essence of Smart Money Habits

The financial landscape for women is unique, threaded with challenges and triumphs. Smart money habits for women mean creating a cushion against life's uncertainties while paving a path to personal goals. It's about making proactive choices—like Sophia, who started a small savings plan that turned into a robust emergency fund, allowing her to make career choices without financial panic.

Living Within Means: A Celebration, not a Constraint

Living within your means is not a shackle but a strategy for growth. It's a conscious decision to avoid the pitfalls of debt and the allure of credit, just as Jenna did when she carefully budgeted her way to a debt-free life after her divorce.

Practical Strategies for Women

- Identifying Income and Expenses: Understand that managing money isn't necessarily about earning more but optimizing what you have—like Maria, who juggled two jobs and learned to track every penny, finding freedom within her budget.

Crafting a Budget: It's about creating a plan that accommodates both dreams and responsibilities. Women, like Ana, who balanced her family's needs with her aspirations, crafted a budget that supported her children's education and her entrepreneurial ventures.

Risk Management: Fortifying Against Life's Surprises

Life is unpredictable, but our finances don't have to be. Investing in contingency funds and insurance, like Leah did after her health scare, ensures that emergencies don't derail your financial stability.

Generating Returns: Building a Legacy

Making money work for you is about smart investments—like Rachel, who started small with stock investments, which grew over time to become a substantial part of her retirement plan.

The Difference Between Earning and Making Money

Earning money is an active endeavor; making money is letting your investments do the work. It's the shift from being an employee to becoming an investor, a transition that Elena embraced as she started her own business while investing in income-generating assets.

In the next pages, we will explore the how and why of these habits, drawing from the wisdom of women who've walked this path. Their stories are our guideposts, their lessons our blueprint for success. As we delve into the world of smart money habits, remember: This is not just about accumulating wealth—it's about claiming your independence, seizing control, and crafting a life of financial confidence.

Smart Money Habits Checklist

Smart money habits are the bedrock of sound financial management. They are the daily routines, principles, and decisions that shape our financial well-being and prepare us to navigate life's economic challenges.

Embrace these habits to pave your way to financial success:

Track Your Spending: Begin by recording all your expenses. Awareness is the first step toward control.

Spend Mindfully: Before making a purchase, ask yourself if it aligns with your financial goals and values.

Budget for Balance: Create a budget that reflects your income, expenses, and financial objectives, ensuring each dollar serves a purpose.

Save Strategically: Aim to save a portion of your income regularly, no matter how small. Over time, these savings can grow significantly.

Embrace Frugality: Living within your means doesn't mean depriving yourself; it means making the most of what you have.

Review Income Sources: Clearly understand where your money comes from and look for opportunities to diversify your income.

Plan for the Unexpected: Set aside funds for emergencies to ensure you're prepared for any financial surprises.

Invest in Your Future: Allocate a portion of your savings to investments that will grow over time, contributing to your long-term wealth.

By adopting these smart money habits, you set the stage for a future where financial stress is minimized, and financial freedom is within reach.

Notes

Quote
/kwōt/

"Financial independence is about having more choices."
Ellevest CEO and Wall Street veteran Sallie Krawcheck

CHAPTER 2

The Power of Setting Goals – A Woman's Vision for Prosperity

"Financial intelligence is not about how much money you have, but about how you manage and plan with the money you have." – Inspired by Daymond John.

The Journey to Financial Goals

Have you ever felt that despite your best efforts, the discipline of smart money management seems just out of reach? Or perhaps you're diligently working, but tangible financial results seem elusive. This chapter is your compass, designed to guide you through setting and achieving meaningful financial goals.

Crafting Financial Goals: The Women's Edition

For women, financial goals are more than figures in a bank account; they are the milestones on the path to autonomy and security. They range from the immediate, such as creating an emergency fund, to the aspirational, such as investing for a child's future or planning for a well-deserved retirement.

Embracing Financial Goals with Intention

Setting financial goals is the cornerstone of wealth creation. Studies show that regardless of income levels, individuals with clear financial targets fare better than those without. As women, our financial goals give us direction, inspiring us to allocate our resources with intention and foresight.

Defining Financial Goals: A Personal Blueprint

To set a financial goal, you must first understand its dimensions. Answer these questions with your vision in mind:
- Who? Me/Us.
- What? Accumulate $10,000.
- When? In 2 years.
- Where? In a high-yield savings account.
- Why? To fund my dream of starting a small business.

The SMART Way: Tailored for Her Financial Growth

SMART goals are not just smart; they're essential. They provide a clear framework for financial decision-making. Here's how to tailor them to your unique journey:
- **Specific:** Clarify your goals. Instead of a vague desire for wealth, pinpoint exactly what financial success looks like to you.

- **Measurable:** Assign numbers to your dreams. If you aim to reduce debt, specify the amount and track your progress.
- **Achievable: Set realistic deadlines.** If you're planning to pay off a student loan, calculate a monthly payment plan that stretches you but is attainable.
- **Relevant:** Make your financial goals resonate with your personal aspirations. Your goals should reflect your values and the life you envision.
- **Time-Bound: Anchor your goals in time.** A goal without a deadline is just a wish. Set dates that propel you to action.

Implementing Goals: A Woman's Strategy
- Create and adhere to a budget that reflects your goals.
- Prioritize building an emergency fund to weather life's uncertainties.
- Pay off debts systematically to liberate your future earnings.
- Invest in your retirement; your future self will thank you.

- Embrace frugality not as a sacrifice, but as a strategic choice for long-term abundance.

A Woman's Financial Commitment

As you navigate through life's various roles—be it as a mother, a professional, an entrepreneur, or all of these—your financial goals serve as your roadmap. By being intentional with every dollar, you empower yourself to not only meet but exceed your aspirations, forging a legacy of prosperity and wisdom.

Financial Goals Setting Checklist

Setting clear financial goals is the cornerstone of building a future you can look forward to with confidence. Here's how to clarify your financial targets and work systematically towards achieving them:

Define Your Financial Goals: Start by precisely articulating what you want to achieve with your money. Whether it's saving for a new car, investing for retirement, or setting aside money for education, clarity is key.

Quantify Your Goals: Attach a specific number to each goal. Determine how much you need to save, invest, or pay off in debt.

Set a Timeline: Assign a realistic yet ambitious timeline for each goal. Break down your timeline into actionable steps with mini-deadlines.

Choose the Right Savings or Investment Vehicle: Decide where to allocate your funds for each goal. For retirement, an IRA might be suitable, while a high-yield savings account could be better for short-term goals.

Understand Your 'Why': Clearly state why each goal is important to you. This will keep you motivated and committed to your plan.

Craft a Workable Budget: Create a budget that balances your income with your expenses and savings goals.

Establish an Emergency Fund: Prioritize building an emergency fund that covers 3-6 months of living expenses.

Eliminate Debt: Develop a plan to pay off existing debts and strategies to stay debt-free.

Plan for Retirement: Regularly contribute to a retirement account to ensure future financial security.

Adopt a Saving Mindset: Aim to save a portion of your income routinely. Look for opportunities to cut back on spending without sacrificing quality of life.

By following this checklist, you'll not only be setting goals but also creating a pathway to achieve them, ensuring that every financial decision moves you closer to your aspirations.

Notes

Quote

/kwōt/

"Setting goals is the first step in turning the invisible into the visible."
Tony Robbins, reinterpreted by Carrie Schwab-Pomerantz

CHAPTER 3

The Wise Way to Budget – A Guided Approach for Women

"A big part of financial freedom is having your heart and mind free from worry about the what-ifs of life."
– Suze Orman

Embracing Budgeting as a Lifeline

Is there a secret to effective budgeting? The answer is a resounding yes, and it lies within the grasp of every woman who seeks to master her finances. Budgeting is not just about keeping track of numbers—it's a strategic skill that can transform your life. It is the scaffolding that supports your dreams, from home ownership to healthcare, and entrepreneurship education.

Understanding the Power of a Budget

Budgeting is about setting priorities and making empowered choices. It's a tool that helps you align your spending with your life's true necessities. Take Michelle, a healthcare worker, who by adhering to a carefully crafted budget, navigated through the financial turmoil of unexpected medical bills without sacrificing her family's well-being.

Crafting a Budget with Realistic Goals

Setting savings goals is the cornerstone of any budget. Whether it's for home repairs, an investment fund, or a much-needed vacation, budgeting lets you prioritize your financial targets. Like Sandra, who through budgeting, managed to save for her daughter's education while funding her own startup, your budget is the blueprint for your financial aspirations.

Tracking Expenses: The First Step to Financial Clarity

By categorizing your spending into discretionary, variable, and fixed expenses, you gain clarity. Jessica, for instance, used a simple budgeting app to track her spending habits, discovering ways to save for a down payment on her first home.

Managing Monthly Income: A Balanced Approach

Knowing what you earn and spend each month is crucial. Record your income meticulously, including all sources such as dividends or side hustles, just as Olivia did when she transitioned to freelancing, ensuring her financial stability.

Evaluating Spending: A Revelation

Assessing your spending patterns can be enlightening. Laura found that by cutting back on daily luxuries, she could redirect funds towards more fulfilling experiences, like a weekend retreat or a professional development course.

Creating and Adjusting Your Budget

The act of creating a budget is transformative. It allows you to allocate your income towards your needs while saving for the future. Revisiting and adjusting your budget regularly, as Maria did after her promotion, ensures that your financial plan grows with you.

The 50/30/20 Rule: Simplifying Budgeting

The 50/30/20 rule offers a simple yet effective framework for organizing your budget:

- 50% Needs: Allocate half of your income to essential expenses such as housing, food, and transportation.
- 30% Wants: Designate thirty percent to personal desires, allowing you to enjoy life's pleasures responsibly.

- **20% Savings:** Commit twenty percent to savings, securing your financial future with an emergency fund and investments.

By integrating this rule into your budgeting practice, you, like Emma, can balance living in the present while

Budgeting: The Path to Smart Money Habits

Mastering the art of budgeting is about more than just numbers—it's about being intentional with your financial decisions. It's a commitment to creating and maintaining smart money habits that forge a path to financial independence.

The Wise Way To Budget Checklist

Budgeting wisely is about more than numbers—it's about crafting a financial plan that supports your life's vision. Follow these steps to create a budget that's both sustainable and aligned with your financial goals:

Clarify Your Savings Goals: Define clear, attainable goals for what you're saving towards, such as an emergency fund or a down payment on a home.

Monitor Your Spending: Keep a detailed log of your expenses. Understanding where your money goes is the first step in taking control of your finances.

Income Tracking: Record your total monthly income from all sources to gain a full picture of your financial resources.

Evaluate Luxuries and Indulgences: Take a look at your discretionary spending and decide where you can cut back without sacrificing your joy.

Draft a Personalized Budget: Develop a budget that fits your unique situation, incorporating your fixed and variable expenses, as well as savings and investments.

Apply the 50/30/20 Strategy: Allocate your income by following the 50/30/20 rule—50% for needs, 30% for wants, and 20% for savings.

Mind the Minor Expenses: It's often the small, recurring expenses that cumulatively impact your budget the most. Keep them in check.

By adhering to this checklist, you're not just following a budget; you're embracing a philosophy of financial wisdom that will serve you throughout your life.

Notes

Quote
/kwōt/

"Wealth is the ability to fully experience life".
Henry David Thoreau

CHAPTER 4

Strategic Saving – A Woman's Guide to Building Wealth

"It's simple arithmetic: Your income can grow only to the extent that you do." — T. Harv Eker

The Art of Saving: A Woman's Perspective

Saving is a journey, not a destination, and like any journey, it starts with a single step. While it may seem daunting at first, especially when life throws curveballs, the payoff is not just in the numbers—it's in the security and options that savings provide. This chapter is dedicated to demystifying the process of saving and showing you, step by step, how to build a robust financial cushion.

Recording Your Expenses: The First Step to Understanding

The foundation of strategic saving is understanding where your money goes. Like Jennifer, who after her divorce had to take a hard look at her finances, you may find that recording every expenditure reveals surprising insights. Whether you use an app or old-fashioned pen and paper, what matters is that you start.

Making Saving a Non-Negotiable Part of Your Budget

A budget isn't just a list of expenses; it's your financial biography. For Elizabeth, a single mother balancing a career and two kids, making saving a fixed part of her budget was non-negotiable. She started small, aiming to save 10% of her income, and gradually increased it, showing her children the value of financial prudence.

Identifying Areas to Cut Back

Cutting back doesn't mean cutting out joy. It means prioritizing what brings you lasting happiness over fleeting pleasures. Consider Laura's story: by choosing to cook at home more often, she saved enough to take her family on a memorable vacation.

Setting Goals: The Milestones of Your Financial Narrative

Goals give saving a purpose. Whether it's an emergency fund or a down payment for your dream home, having clear targets is key. Think of Rachel, who set up a savings goal for a certification course that propelled her career forward.

Prioritizing Your Savings: What Matters Most to You

Determining your financial priorities is about aligning your money with your values. Maria knew that her car was on its last legs, so she started saving for a replacement long before the 'check engine' light came on.

Choosing the Right Saving Tools

Not all savings accounts are created equal. For short-term goals, a high-yield savings account might suffice, but for long-term goals like your child's college fund, consider an IRA or a 529 plan. Emily, a freelance writer, diversified her savings tools to match her goals, ensuring her money worked as hard as she did.

Automating Your Savings: Set It and Forget It

Automatic transfers are like financial autopilots. By setting up her savings to transfer automatically, Sophie could focus on growing her online business, secure in the knowledge that her savings were growing too.

Monitoring Your Savings: Celebrate Your Progress
Saving is an active process. By regularly reviewing her savings, Anita could adjust her strategies, celebrate successes, and address any shortcomings, keeping her financial goals on track.

Embracing the Power of Strategic Saving
Strategic saving isn't just about accumulating wealth; it's about claiming your future. It's a declaration of your independence and a commitment to yourself and your family. As you embark on your strategic saving journey, remember that each dollar saved is a building block for your dream life.

Strategic Saving Checklist

True, saving isn't always easy, but it's a rewarding journey with the right plan in place. Follow these steps to save with purpose and build a financial cushion that can withstand economic fluctuations:

Monitor Your Spending: Keep a detailed account of all your expenditures. Knowing where your money goes is essential for effective saving.

Incorporate Savings into Your Budget: Treat your savings like a fixed expense. Allocate a portion of your income to savings each month as you would with any other non-negotiable bill.

Identify Opportunities to Reduce Costs: Examine your spending to find areas where you can cut back, such as dining out less or canceling unused subscriptions.

Establish Clear Saving Objectives: Set specific, measurable saving goals, both short-term and long-term, to guide your saving strategy.

Prioritize Your Savings: Ascertain which financial goals are most important to you and allocate your savings accordingly.

Choose Suitable Saving Instruments: Research and select the best saving tools for your needs, such as high-yield savings accounts, certificates of deposit, or investment accounts.

Automate Your Savings: Set up automatic transfers to your savings account to ensure consistent savings without the need for manual intervention.

By adopting this structured approach to saving, you'll find that saving money becomes less about challenging self-restraint and more about establishing a secure financial habit that pays off in the long run.

Notes

Quote
/kwōt/

"You are only one decision away from a completely different life".
Mel Robbins

CHAPTER 5

Investing for The Future – A Woman's Financial Empowerment

"In fact, what determines your wealth is not how much you make but how much you keep of what you make." — David Bach, reimagined for the savvy woman investor.

The Joy of Growing Your Wealth

While it's tempting to live in the moment, enjoying the fruits of our hard work immediately, true financial empowerment comes from looking ahead. It's not about how much we earn but about planning and investing for the future. This chapter is about moving beyond the paycheck-to-paycheck existence to create a financial buffer that can withstand life's uncertainties.

Investing: A Commitment to Your Future Self

Investing is more than a financial strategy; it's a commitment to your future self. It's about making choices today that will support your well-being tomorrow. It's not just for the wealthy or the well-versed in the stock market—it's for every woman who wants more out of life than just making ends meet.

Why Invest? A Woman's Perspective

The "precautionary motive" for investing is about safeguarding against life's unexpected turns. For example, when Laura's car broke down unexpectedly, her investment in a rainy-day fund turned a potential crisis into a manageable inconvenience.

Investing for specific purposes is about being goal-oriented. Whether it's saving for your child's college education, as Maria did, or setting aside funds for a much-needed family vacation, allocating money toward these goals can bring them within reach.

Wealth accumulation is about creating the life you want. For Ana, it was about building a nest egg that allowed her to take a sabbatical and travel the world—a dream she had nurtured for years.

The Investment Planning Process: A Structured Approach

- Start fresh, without being hindered by past experiences.
- Link your investment plans to your life goals, like Sofia, who aligned her investments with her passion for a sustainable lifestyle.

- Prioritize your goals, understanding that not everything can be achieved at once but each step forward counts.
- Regularly review your investment plan, adapting as life changes, just as Emma did when she became a mother.
- Embed investment activities into your routine. Setting up automatic contributions can make investing as habitual as your morning coffee.

Investing in Your Financial Future

Investing for the future involves more than just traditional options like stocks and bonds—it's about making holistic decisions that encompass all aspects of your life.

Start a retirement fund early. The sooner you begin, the more you benefit from compound interest, as was the case for Zoe, who started her IRA in her twenties and watched it grow exponentially.

Set clear financial goals. Determine both short-term and long-term objectives and measure your progress against them. For Chloe, this meant setting up a monthly savings goal to eventually open her own bakery.

Growing Your Savings: The Path to Prosperity

Growing your savings is about making your money work for you. Whether it's through CDs, money market accounts, or high-yield savings accounts, the key is to choose the right vehicle for your goals and comfort level.

Beyond finances, investing in your health, career, and relationships is just as crucial. Nourishing your body, advancing your career, and cherishing time with loved ones are investments that yield immeasurable returns.

Conclusion

Investing is a powerful act of self-care. It's about making informed choices today that will secure your tomorrow. By embracing the strategies outlined in this chapter, you're not just investing money; you're investing in a future where your dreams and financial security are one and the same.

Investing For the Future Checklist

While the temptation to live solely in the present is strong, wise investing is about securing your future financial well-being. Let's adopt a strategy that

Investing for the Future Checklist

While the temptation to live solely in the present is strong, wise investing is about securing your future financial well-being. Let's adopt a strategy that ensures you can enjoy your earnings now while also building for tomorrow:

Initiate a Retirement Plan: Prioritize starting your retirement savings. Whether it's an IRA, 401(k), or another pension plan, begin contributing now to reap the benefits of compound interest.

Clarify Financial Ambitions: Define what you're working toward. Set clear, actionable financial goals for both the near and distant future and map out a path to achieve them.

Establish a Rainy-Day Fund: Begin setting aside a portion of your income for unexpected expenses. This fund serves as your financial umbrella, keeping you covered during life's downpours.

Expand Your Savings: Look beyond traditional savings accounts. Explore options like high-yield accounts, CDs, or bonds to grow your savings more effectively.

By following these steps, you're actively building a robust financial foundation that will support you through every stage of life.

Notes

Quote
/kwōt/

"Building wealth is a marathon, not a sprint. Discipline is the key ingredient."
Abigail Johnson, CEO of Fidelity Investments.

CHAPTER 6

Making Your Money Work for You – A Woman's Guide to Financial Independence

"*Do not save what is left after spending, but spend what is left after saving.*" – Warren Buffett, adapted as a mantra for women who aspire to financial freedom.

The Power of Passive Income

Financial liberation is not just about the income you actively earn; it's about creating streams of income that flow even when you're not working. This chapter is dedicated to teaching you the art of making money work for you, an essential step toward financial independence for women everywhere.

Understanding Earning vs. Making Money

Earning money is the active pursuit—trading your time and skills for pay. But there comes a time when you must shift from earning to making money—where your investments return income without the constant exchange of your time. This transition from earning to making money is what sets the stage for lasting financial autonomy.

Strategies for Making Money
To truly make money, consider passive income

avenues like dividend-producing stocks or rental properties. Imagine Lisa, who started with a modest investment in a rental property that now generates regular income, supplementing her day job.

Expanding Your Savings Portfolio
A traditional savings account can provide a stable but limited return. Diversifying into bonds or dividend stocks, as Emily did, can increase your earnings over time. Remember, the key is patience and a clear understanding of your financial instruments.

Planning for Retirement: Your Future Self's Foundation
Retirement planning is about ensuring you have a reliable income when you're no longer working. It's never too early to start, as demonstrated by Sophia, who began contributing to her 401(k) in her first job, benefiting from her company's match program.

Leveraging Resources: Multiplying Your Financial Potential
Leverage involves using resources, such as loans or

partnerships, to increase your investment potential.

For instance, Ava used a small loan to buy a piece of real estate, turning it into a profitable rental property.

Investing in Yourself: The Ultimate Financial Strategy

Remember, investing isn't just about money. It's about investing in your education, your health, and your relationships. As you grow, so does your ability to generate wealth. Consider Tara, who took an online course that led to a lucrative side business.

Conclusion: Your Money, Your Power

Your financial journey is unique, and so is your path to making your money work for you. Whether it's through savvy investments, smart savings, or leveraging opportunities, the goal is to achieve the freedom to live on your terms. The principles outlined in this chapter are not just strategies; they're the tools to build the life you envision.

Making Your Money Work for You Checklist

Creating a financial system that earns for you even when you're not at work is essential for lasting financial security. Here's how to ensure your money continues to grow:

　　Diversify Your Savings: Look beyond basic savings accounts. Consider bonds, high-yield accounts, and other savings instruments that work harder for you.

　　Establish a Robust Retirement Plan: Contribute to a retirement fund such as an IRA or 401(k). The goal is to build a nest egg that will provide for you when you're no longer working.

　　Utilize Leverage Wisely: Use leverage, such as loans or mortgages, to invest in assets that will generate income, like real estate or a business venture.

　　Invest in Income-Generating Instruments: Place your funds into vehicles like dividend-paying stocks, bonds, or mutual funds that can provide a steady stream of income.

By implementing these strategies, you ensure that your money is not just idly sitting but actively working and multiplying, securing not just your current financial situation but also your future.

Notes

Quote
/kwōt/

"An investment in knowledge pays the best interest."
Sallie Krawcheck

CHAPTER 7

Mindful Spending - Nurturing Financial Awareness for Women

"Without values, goals rarely get accomplished... Values are the key. When you understand them correctly, they will pull you toward your dreams — which is a lot more effective than having to push yourself!" — David Bach, adapted for the mindful spender.

Embracing Mindful Spending

Mindful spending isn't about restriction; it's about making every dollar a deliberate step toward your dreams. Whether it's for gratification or necessity, every purchase should align with your values and goals. This chapter is about transforming your spending habits to support a life of financial balance and well-being.

Mindful Spending 101

Creating and sticking to a budget is just the beginning. True financial management comes from being mindful about where your money goes. It's about making conscious choices with your spending, just like Angela, who learned to enjoy life's pleasures without jeopardizing her financial goals.

Crafting a Conscious Spending Plan

To spend mindfully is to spend intentionally. Begin with a 'buy list' and a cooling-off period for purchases, as Clara did when she saved for her dream vacation without accruing debt.

Understanding Your Spending Triggers

Recognizing why and when you spend is crucial. Like Emma, who discovered her online shopping increased when she felt stressed, identifying your triggers can help you avoid impulsive spending.

Tracking Every Expense

Knowing where your money goes gives you control over your financial narrative. For Sophia, tracking her expenses was eye-opening, leading her to make smarter choices that aligned with her long-term aspirations.

Using Cash to Foster Awareness

The tactile experience of using cash, as Maria found, can make the act of parting with money more significant, helping to curb mindless spending.

Allocating Every Dollar with Purpose

A zero-sum budget, where every dollar has a job, helped Rachel focus her resources on what truly mattered to her, from emergency funds to entertainment.

Pocket Money: Financial Autonomy in Practice

Having personal pocket money allowed Laura to enjoy her hobbies without affecting her family's budget, striking a balance between independence and responsibility.

Setting Specific Spending Goals

Reducing spending in specific categories, like dining out, can have a significant impact. Julia's experience of cutting back on restaurant meals helped her contribute more to her retirement fund.

Choosing Value Over Cost

Opting for experiences that offer value rather than just low cost can enrich your life without breaking the bank. Lily's choice to enjoy free local concerts over expensive shows is a prime example of this principle.

The Journey to Mindful Spending

As you embark on this journey of mindful spending, remember that it's about more than just saving money — it's about creating a life that reflects your deepest values and aspirations. With dedication and mindfulness, you'll find that your financial life enriches your whole world.

Mindful Spending Checklist

Embracing mindful spending is about making every financial decision count towards your well-being and goals. Here's how to practice mindful spending in your daily life:

Reflect Before You Buy: Implement a waiting period for all non-essential purchases to differentiate between 'wants' and 'needs'.

Identify Spending Triggers: Recognize situations or emotions that prompt you to spend unnecessarily and develop strategies to avoid or manage them.

Regularly Track Your Spending: Use a budgeting app or a simple spreadsheet to record all your expenses, no matter how small.

Use Cash for Discretionary Spending: Limit your discretionary spending by only using cash, which can help curb impulse purchases.

Set Clear Financial Intentions: Write down your

Mindful Spending Checklist

spending intentions for each category of your budget to maintain focus on your priorities.

Allocate Funds with Purpose Using the 50/30/20 Rule: Structure your budget with 50% for needs, 30% for wants, and 20% for savings and investments.

Scrutinize Small, Recurring Costs: Evaluate your subscriptions and habitual small purchases that can add up over time.

By integrating these steps into your financial routine, you'll cultivate a habit of spending with intention, aligning your financial actions with your long-term objectives and values.

Notes

Quote

/kwōt/

"Money is a tool. Used wisely, it creates an opportunity for a life with choices that reflect your values."

Jean Chatzky, financial journalist, and author.

CHAPTER 8

Building Multiple Income Streams – A Woman's Path to Financial Resilience

"Success is the sum of small efforts, repeated day in and day out." — Robert Collier, echoed for the modern woman seeking financial stability and growth.

The Essentiality of Income Diversification

As we conclude our journey through smart money habits, we come to a crucial strategy: diversifying your income. In today's volatile economy, relying on a single source of income is akin to walking a tightrope without a safety net. This chapter is not just about building wealth; it's about creating a financial ecosystem that can weather any storm.

The Case for Multiple Streams of Income

Imagine you're a gardener. Just as you wouldn't plant only one type of seed, you shouldn't rely on one type of income. Diversification is your hedge against uncertainty. It provides stability and the freedom to pursue your passions and interests without financial constraints.

Creating a Symphony of Income Streams

- Dividend Income: It's the quiet, consistent performer in your financial orchestra. Investing in dividend-yielding stocks or funds, as Laura did, provides her with a steady rhythm of passive income that complements her active earnings.
- Rental Income: Like owning a fertile plot of land, rental properties can yield a bountiful harvest. Sarah diversified her income with a small apartment building, providing her with a steady cash flow that funds her non-profit work.
- Earned Income: Your daily work is the melody that carries you forward. By incorporating side hustles, like Emily's graphic design freelance work, you can add variations to your financial tune.
- Royalties: Compose a masterpiece once, and let it play on repeat. Rachel wrote a series of e-books that continue to generate royalties, a testament to the enduring power of creativity.

- **Business Income:** Whether it's a product-based Etsy store like Anita's or a service-oriented consulting firm like Priya's, owning a business is like directing your own financial symphony.
- **Interest Income:** The gentle hum in the background, interest income from bonds and high-yield savings accounts, supports your financial chorus without stealing the spotlight.

Bonus Tracks: Extra Ways to Earn
- From starting a lifestyle blog, like Jessica, that turned into a full-time career, to driving for a ride-sharing service, like Maria, on weekends to fund her art projects, the possibilities are endless. Offering online courses, freelancing, or virtual assistance are all modern variations on the theme of income diversification.

Conducting Your Financial Future

As we close the book on our smart money habits series, remember that building multiple income streams is about more than just money—it's about crafting a life of choice, security, and abundance. Start small, be consistent, and watch as your financial garden grows into a diverse, flourishing landscape that sustains you through all seasons of life.

Building Multiple Income Streams Checklist

Diversifying your income is essential in a world where financial stability is key. Here's how to broaden your income sources and solidify your financial security:

Start a Niche Blog: Share your expertise or passion online. A successful blog can generate income through ads, affiliate marketing, and sponsored content.

Seek Investment Opportunities: Even small investments can yield returns over time. Consider low-cost index funds or peer-to-peer lending platforms.

Offer Your Skills on Fiverr: Whether it's graphic design or copywriting, market your skills on platforms like Fiverr to earn money on a freelance basis.

Freelance Writing: Craft articles, blog posts, or web content. Good writers are always in demand.

Become a Virtual Assistant: Assist businesses remotely with tasks ranging from email management to customer service.

Launch a Home-Based Business: Turn a hobby or skill into a business. Home-based businesses reduce overhead costs and offer flexible working hours.

Drive for Ride-Sharing Services: If you have a car, driving for services like Uber can be a flexible way to earn extra money.

Create an Online Course: If you're knowledgeable in a particular area, create a course and sell it on platforms like Udemy or Teachable.

By exploring these avenues, you can create a robust system of income streams that provide financial cushioning and growth opportunities.

Closing Thoughts: Embracing Your Financial Journey

"The habit of saving is itself an education; it fosters every virtue, teaches self-denial, cultivates the sense of order, trains to forethought, and so broadens the mind." --T.T. Munger

As we turn the final page of this journey, remember that smart money habits go beyond mere financial organization—they are the blueprint for building a legacy. It's not just about order in your accounts, but harmony in your life. It's about the conscious discipline that transforms today's sacrifices into tomorrow's freedoms.

You've equipped yourself with more than knowledge; you've started a movement in your life —one that marches steadily towards enduring wealth and wisdom. This is not a path devoid of challenges, but one that is rich with potential and purpose.

Carry with you the dedication to craft smart money habits daily, as these habits are the threads that weave the tapestry of your financial future. With every choice that aligns with your vision board, you're painting the grand picture of your life—one stroke at a time.

In your hands lies the power to sidestep the snares of debt, the allure of impulsive spending, and the uncertainty of the future. With the tools and insights gained, stride confidently towards a horizon of financial prosperity that doesn't just shine for you but illuminates the path for those who follow.

Let your financial vision board be your compass, your unwavering commitment to it, your wind in the sails. And when you look back, years from this moment, you'll see a journey marked by growth, resilience, and success—a testament to the enduring power of smart money habits.

Together, we've started something remarkable. Now, go forth and build a future that echoes with the sound of your achievements.

Quote

/kwōt/

"Financial peace isn't the acquisition of stuff. It's learning to live on less than you make, so you can give money back and have money to invest. You can't win until you do this."
Dave Ramsey

www.ingramcontent.com/pod-product-compliance
Lightning Source LLC
Chambersburg PA
CBHW070400230526
45471CB00006B/2650